Snowflake, Snowflake

Written by Jennifer Barone

Illustrated by Laura Catrinella

How do **snowflakes** form their **beautiful** design while they fall from the **sky**? If I could **catch** them **all** in my **hand**, they would make a delicious **pie**.

Little **white** stars at **dance**,
snowflakes twirl, **spin**
and **prance**.

Look! A single **special** snowflake has **landed** right there on my **mitten**. I call this one **my** very own. I **cradle** it **just** like a **kitten**.

I **lay** my head **back** and
stretch out my **tongue** to
get a **taste**. I **try** to catch them
all, I won't let **them** go to **waste**.

What a **sight** to see on this **cold** winter night. **Millions** of dancing **snowflakes** have created a blanket on the **ground**. They cover this **earth** for miles around.

Snowflake, snowflake so **sweet**, gentle and **pure**. It's **you** that **makes** our world **so** peaceful– **just** like a **cure**.

About the Author

Jennifer was born and raised in Sault Ste. Marie, Ontario. She is an Early Childhood Educator who teaches Kindergarten. As the author of *Goose On A Roof*, her debut book, Jennifer turned to her students as her biggest inspiration to create *Snowflake Snowflake*. She believes we need to find the love and beauty in everything and everyone. She enjoys reading, swimming, an avid yoga enthusiast and spending time with her family and friends. She resides in Sault Ste. Marie, a city where winter is common nearly all year around with her husband Luciano who has always been her greatest support.

FriesenPress

Suite 300 - 990 Fort St
Victoria, BC, V8V 3K2
Canada

www.friesenpress.com

ISBN
978-1-5255-5090-4 (Hardcover)
978-1-5255-5091-1 (Paperback)
978-1-5255-5092-8 (eBook)

1. Juvenile Nonfiction, Curiosities & Wonders

Distributed to the trade by The Ingram Book Company

Lightning Source UK Ltd.
Milton Keynes UK
UKHW051602181019
351585UK00009B/73/P

9 781525 550904